Bill's Bull

Words by Amanda Graham
Illustrated by Greg Holfeld

Bill's bull was ill, ill, ill.
"Call Doctor Ball,"
said Bill to Jill.

3

"His teeth have holes,"
said Doctor Ball.
"I'll drill, then fill.
He'll soon be well."

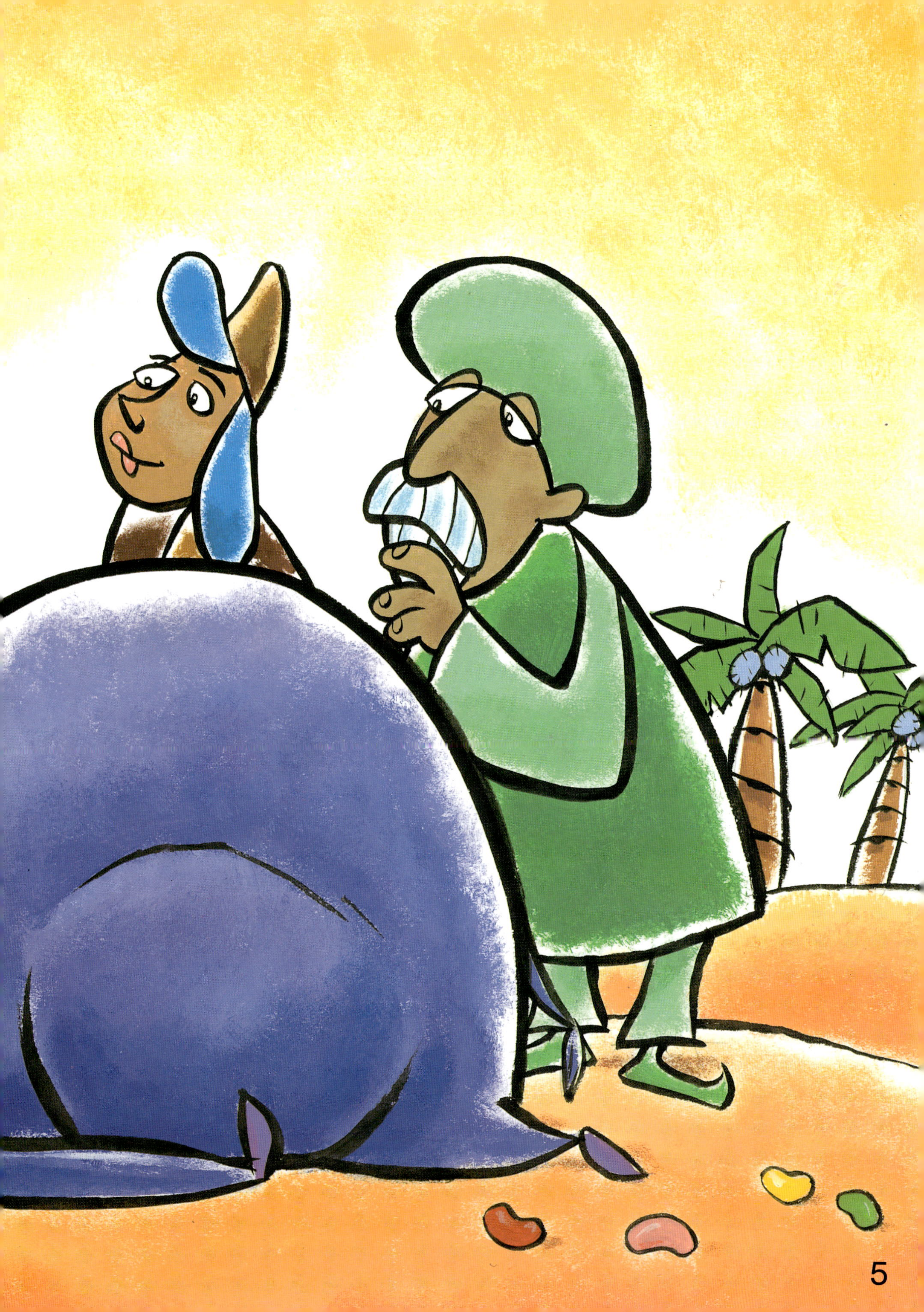

But Bill's bull was still ill.
"Call Doctor Hill,"
said Bill to Jill.

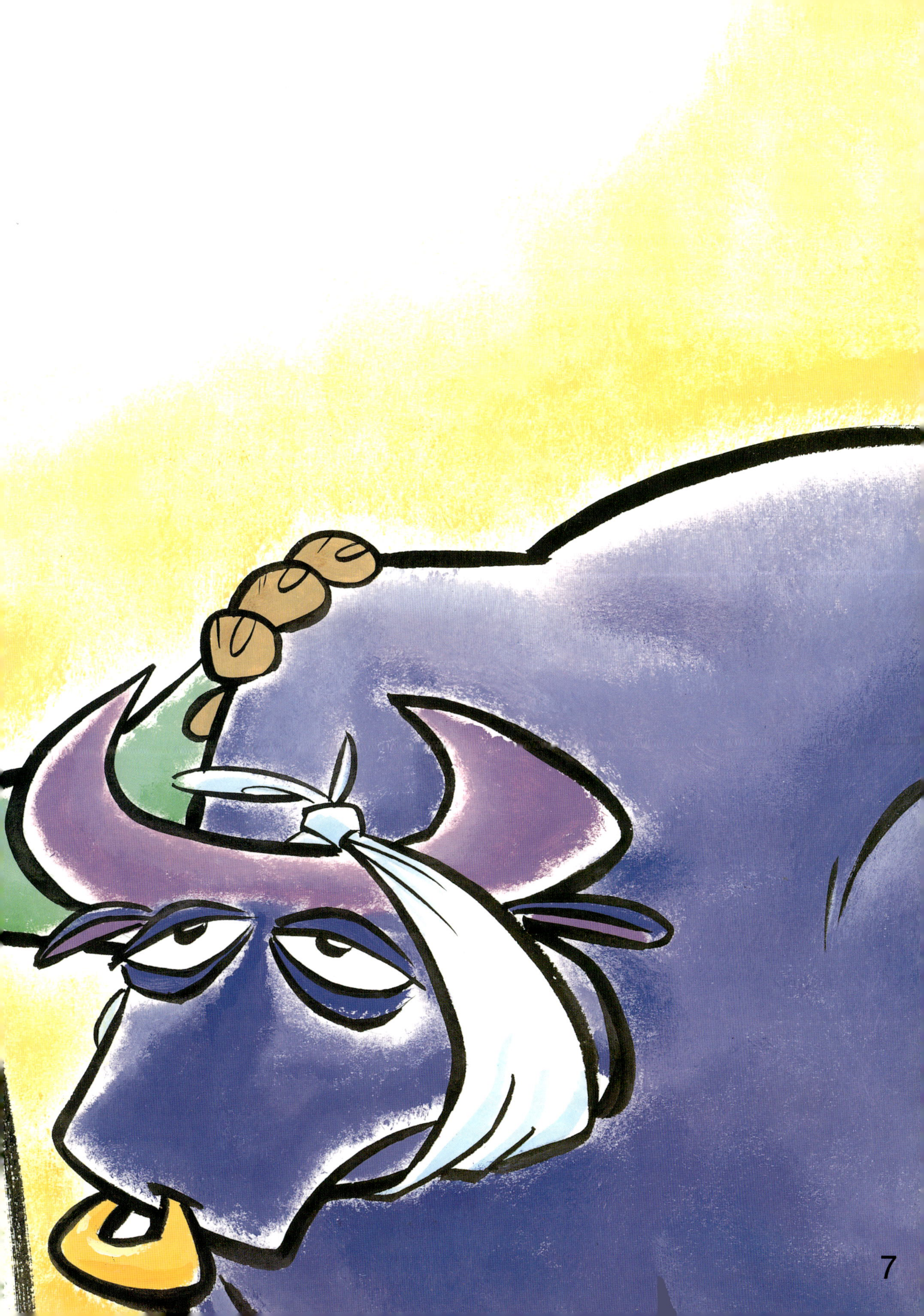

"He has a chill,"
said Doctor Hill.
"Here's a pill.
He'll soon be well."

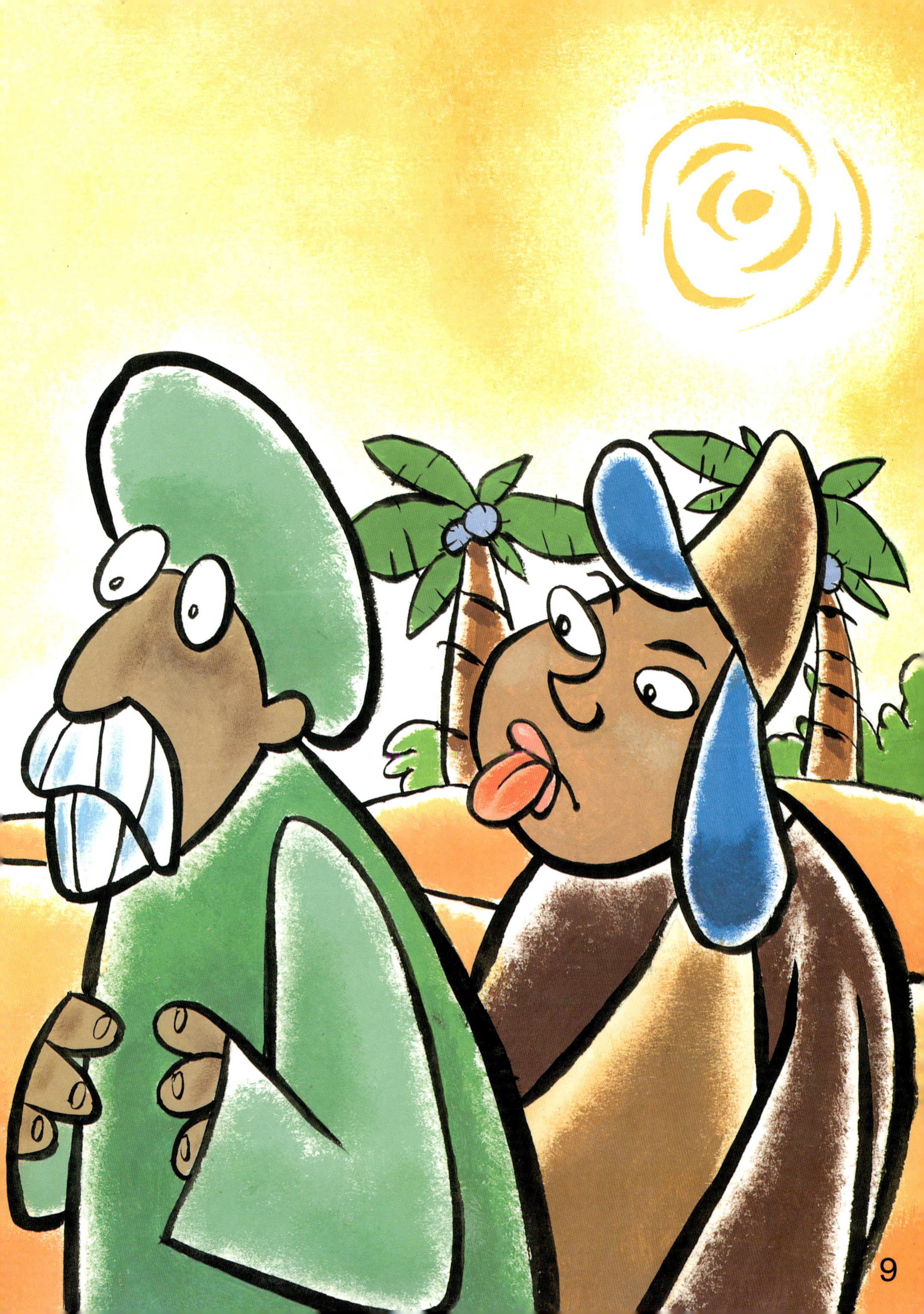

But Bill's bull was still ill.
"Call Doctor Bell," said Bill to Jill.

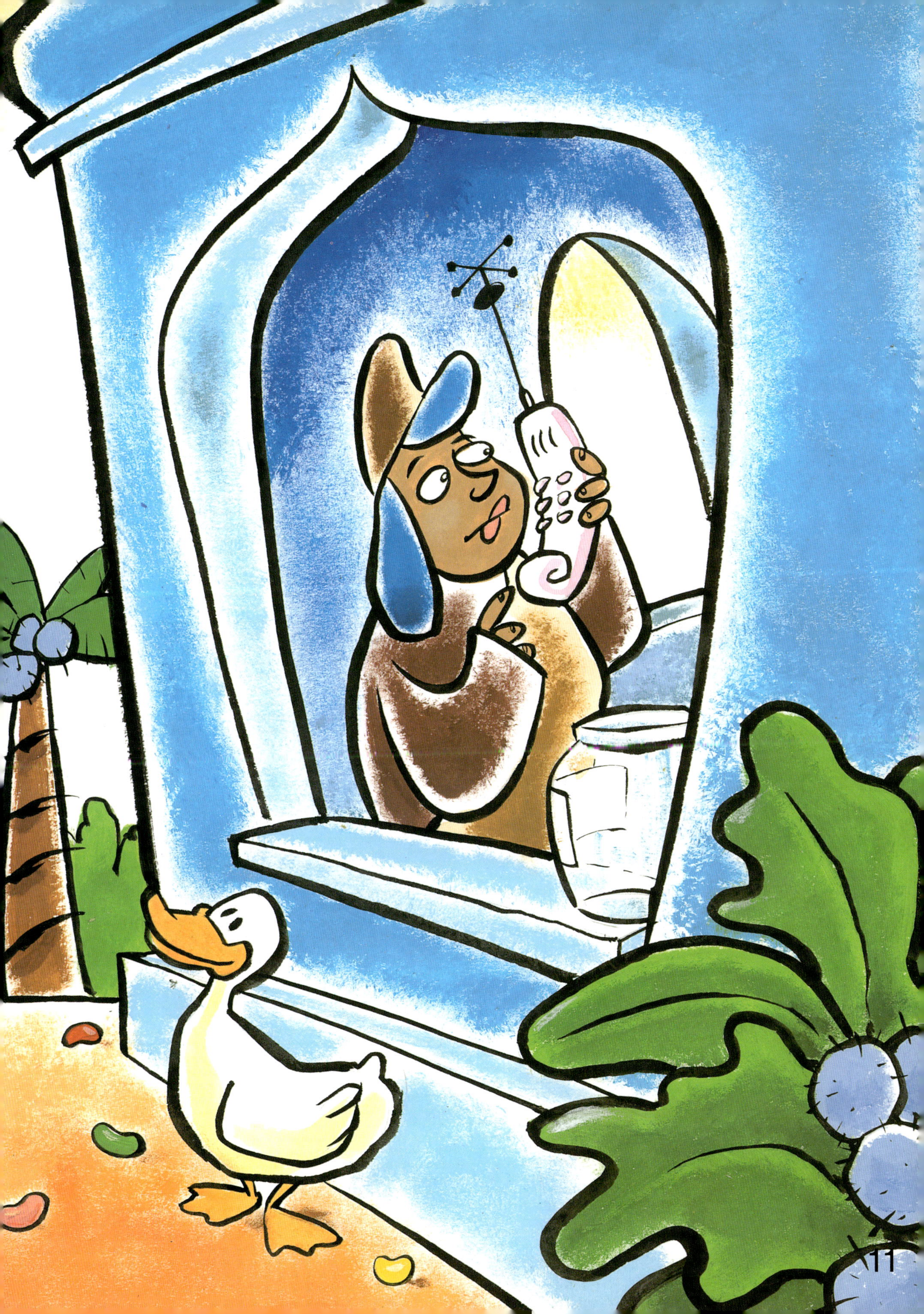

"Just keep him still,"
said Doctor Bell.
"I cannot tell
why he is ill."

But the bull knew
why he was ill, ill, ill.

14 He had a big belly that was

full, full, full

of all Jill's jellybeans.

Greedy old bull.